HEART RHYTHMS,
MIND MELODIES,
AND SO ON...
the song of the soul in poetry

HEART RHYTHMS, MIND MELODIES, AND SO ON...

the song of the soul in poetry

T. H. TESSEMA

Heart rhythms, mind melodies, and so on…:
the song of the soul in poetry.

ISBN-13: 978-1500286316
ISBN-10: 1500286311

First Trade Printing: September 2014
Second Trade Printing: March 2015

Printed in the United States of America

To Love.

TABLE OF CONTENTS

PREFACE

If I could isolate space, and time, and memory, and confine the existence of these to a particular series of moments, then I would say that *HEART RHYTHMS, MIND MELODIES, AND SO ON...: the song of the soul in poetry* is a composition that spans seven years. The simple explanation for the arrival of this collection would be that the selected poems in this work are pieces that I composed between the ages of eighteen and twenty-five years old. They are expressions of moments lived during that time, recollections of moments from the past, and perhaps my longings for future moments. The truth is, however, I do not know if I am able to chronicle this work that easily. I do not know when and where it all began and ended, or if it has ended yet, or if it has really even begun at all. The "it" about which I am speaking is the song that rouses my soul; it is a song which I have found that I am able to communicate, in part, through this art form called poetry.

Poetry is a gift, and I am infinitely grateful that God has granted me permission to hold this gift at this time. I acknowledge each moment that poetry remains with me as my present. When I have felt low and nearly ready to sink into despair, poetry has kept me afloat. When my weary eyes have been almost all set to close on this life, poetry has stirred me awake and tapped me on the shoulder in the sweet whispers of words...
When I am restless, poetry is the lullaby that soothes me. When I am unknowing, poetry is the nursery rhyme that instructs me. When I am lonely, poetry is the lover that serenades me.

If someone had asked me a few years ago, I never would have imagined that the "whispers of words" would grow to become this collection of poetry. When I was writing many of these poems, I was only in search of refuge for my wandering soul. I was in great need of sanctuary, and I found solace in the music emanating from my mind. This solace was, and continues to be, a blessing for me. Now, I am thankful for yet another blessing which emerges in the opportunity to share my song with others...

As I look back on these poems today, I find that they are me, and yet they are not me. Somehow, they are fragments of me that have come, and gone, and arrived. They are all part of my *becoming* – a beauty emerging and evolving. As I believe that we do not live on this earth alone... as I believe that there is a Heavenly force that guides us and unites us... my prayer is that somewhere in these pages... you - the reader, the listener, the audience – will find a part of your song here too.

January 2011

PART ONE
I am a frequent dreamer.

I am a frequent dreamer. I am an avid and active dreamer. Intense, internal visions fill the spaces of my mundane days and nights. They are visions of the past, the present, and the desired future. In these visions, I am yearning and reaching out for so much...: love, peace, joy, understood purpose, reckoning with the past, comfort in the present, and divine instruction for the future. In my visions, my yearnings have the freedom to become my manifested reality. Therefore, if and when I do not witness these harmonious conditions when my eyes are open, I always have them in my dreams...
In this way, I am not unlike many other dreamers.

One morning not so long ago, while I was seizing my final hours of rest before rising for the day, I had such a pleasant dream. It was the kind of dream that fills your soul with ineffable gratitude. I was so overwhelmed by the feeling that this dream produced inside of me that I woke up with tears drizzling down my warm cheeks. The rain was cleansing and reviving, and the showers made me new again.

1

My dreams are always very palpable. My dreams engage all of my senses, and the episodes in them often feel just as veritable as events taking place in my waking hours. I see, I hear, I touch, I smell, I taste. I am completely... in my dreams. I existed in this dream with this kind of perceptibility, and I am able to live it all over again in my memory.

I remember walking out onto the front steps of the house in which I have lived my whole life. It was a sunny, late September morning in Ardmore, Pennsylvania, and summer was holding hands with autumn. I looked out into the desolate, suburban street, knowing my eyes were searching for something... I just stood there for a while in almost absolute silence, and the only noteworthy sound was the occasional murmuring of bumble bees grazing in our front garden. I smelled the wetness of dew-kissed earth, and I tasted a deep hunger in my mouth. I waited, and I waited, until the moment finally came when I caught sight of the one for whom I had been waiting. As her silhouette approached me in the distance, I admit that I did not have immediate recognition of her. So much time had passed, and the memory of her drifted further away from me with each passing year. When I realized who she was, my stomach stirred with butterflies. "That's my old friend", I thought to myself, "and I've missed her dearly."

She was riding up the sidewalk on her little pink and white bicycle with training wheels and rainbow-colored streamers flowing from the handle

2

bars. I examined her as she came toward me. I knew her outfit very well. It was my favorite magenta colored sweat-suit from childhood. The sweatshirt had yellow and white embroidered flowers just below the neckline that resembled daisies. There was a yellow flower in the center, and two white flowers on the shoulders. Just below the daisy-like flowers was a thick strip of white lace encircling the chest, shoulders, and back. My mother, who was – of course – the one who dressed me, coordinated with the sweat-suit by adding a crisp white turtleneck underneath the sweatshirt, white, lace-trimmed socks, and white, high-top sneakers. The finishing touch was the tying of magenta ribbon at the ends of my cottony pig-tails. Although our family lived off a modest income in the early years of my childhood and most of our clothing was purchased from the thrift store, my mom always made sure that my older sister and I were clean and presentable.

In one of our old family photo albums, there is a picture of me wearing this same outfit back in 1989. I am four years old in this photograph. I am outside on the front steps of the house in which I have lived my whole life. It is a sunny day. I don't know what time of year it is, but all I can tell is ... I am happy. Standing no more than three feet high with slender arms and legs, I appear almost delicate to the touch. The sun is sweet on my burnt sienna skin and squinting eyes, and I am grinning at the camera.

In years since, when someone pulls out the old photo albums, I have found myself admiring this

3

particular photo. It is dear to me for many reasons. For one, in my favorite childhood outfit – although it was just a children's playsuit – I always felt quite pretty and dressed up. Perhaps, it was the prettiest that I have ever felt in my whole life. For another, I admire the joy and simplicity that I recall I felt in my early youth. Now, at twenty-five years old, when I'm attempting to comprehend adulthood, I admit that sometimes I just want to go back to that time... If I could, just for a moment, go back to that time... when my biggest decision was whether I wanted Mommy to fix me peanut butter and jelly or grilled cheese for lunch...when ants crawling on my legs as a result of sitting on the wooden coffee table in our living room was my biggest fear... and when I would sing "Memories" and "This Little Light of Mine" and "Amazing Grace" and bang on piano keys without shame in front of elderly people at the senior citizens' center where my mother used to work. Or, maybe I would like to go back to the time when riding my bicycle with training wheels up and down the street – while Mommy or Daddy closely watched my every move – was the most exciting activity I had ever known...

I have recently taken up bike riding as a hobby again. Now, the training wheels are off, I ride for miles instead of a few feet down the street, and I do not see Mommy and Daddy right there beside me. I realize that I am riding because I am in pursuit of that same feeling that I had when I was young. I

4

want to know that same freedom… but I also want to know that same security.

When I saw my old friend, I felt such a feeling of completeness at our reunion. As she was so captured by the merriment of riding her bike, she did not even notice me at first. I wanted to hug her, hold her hand, or at least say hello. My old friend zoomed past me up the street, and then back down the street again. Then she rode up and down the street over, and over, and over again. I do not know how many times she repeated this pattern. All I know is that I just fixed my eyes on her as she was making her revolutions. Then, on her last go-round….she finally turned, and looked at me. Our eyes intertwined, and we were one again. She grinned that same buoyant grin that I remember in that old photograph from when I was four years old. Feeling like a thousand clouds were underneath my feet, I smiled back at her.

As she approached me this last time, she started to slow down. When she arrived in front of me, she stopped her bike, extended her arm, and I understood that she was welcoming me to touch her hand. I reached out my hand in kind, and our fingertips caressed. In that moment, there was so no difference between her season and mine.

Then I blinked, and she sped off down the street. I watched her ride off until her image evaporated in the distance. My old friend was gone, and yet she was still here with me. She had come back to me, and now she would never leave me ever again.

5

I am a frequent dreamer. I am an avid and active dreamer. Intense, internal visions fill the spaces of my mundane days and nights. They are visions of the past, the present, and the desired future. In these visions, I am yearning and reaching out for so much...: love, peace, joy, understood purpose, reckoning with the past, comfort in the present, and divine instruction for the future. In my visions, my yearnings have the freedom to become my manifested reality. Therefore, if and when I do not witness these harmonious conditions when my eyes are open, I always have them in my dreams...
In this way, I am not unlike many other dreamers.

September 2010

PART TWO
When She Sings...

1.

The Maternal Song

If ever there were a song that I wanted to hear...
it would be the quiet, yet resounding melody of
the moans and groans
of my mothers' souls.
My mother,
my mother's mother,
 my mother's mother's mother,
and all my "othermothers"
who were and are
my aunts, my cousins, and my sisters.
Together they form a line that stretches back
into eternity.
This line is a sound wave
that has traveled through the ages,
and it has progressed in stages.
It has bounced back and forth
through the undercurrents of history.
It is "her story"...the sacred mystery.

7

It is the wisdom
that has mystically
passed through the generations
by umbilical cord.
And through the blood, the water, and the Spirit
that flowed through them and into me,
it has become
my story.

My story —
the sacred mystery is captured in the melody.
It is the melody of the moans and groans
of my mothers' souls.
It is their collective prayers to God Most High.
It is their constant praise
even on the weariest days.
It is the Wisdom that teaches
that "trouble doesn't last always".

The sacred mystery is the song of...
"survival".

I listen closely,
and I hear the song
 in the rhythms of my beating heart
 in the pumping and flowing of my blood,
in the echoes of each breath,
and in the whispers of my anticipating womb.

If ever there were a song that I wanted to hear...
it would be the loud and resounding melody
of the joy in my daughters' souls.
My daughter, my daughter's daughter,
 my daughter's daughter's daughter,
and all my "otherdaughters"
who are and will be
my nieces, my cousins, and my sisters.
Together they will form a line
that will progress forward
into eternity.

Then... I will witness
that my mothers
never sang
their song
in vain.

2.

Enduring Spirit

She is an enduring spirit.

She whispers through the air,
and like a consecrated prayer
she moves through the atmosphere invisibly.
She is unseen,
yet she exists indivisibly.

She is whole –
a solid entity,
yet her identity is represented in parts.
Her personality
is the reality
manifested in the
intricate and diverse
details of the universe.
She is an enduring spirit.
Her breath is the eternal wind,
and all of creation
is the nation
produced from the womb of her lungs.

She is an enduring spirit,
and her name is
life.

3.

A Long Walk with My Sisters

I have taken
a long walk with my sisters.
From the journey,
I have cultivated bruises and blisters.
I share these wounds with them,
and this mutual suffering unites us.
And without this voyage,

I would have never learned...
and I would have never earned
the right to say
that I am
a Woman.

I have taken a long walk with my sisters.
I allow myself to stand in their shoes.
My feet ache from breaking them in,
but I still choose
to recover and retell their story.

I do not neglect it.
I protect it,
and I consider it a sacred memory.

I sympathize.
I empathize.
I synthesize...

and the process
becomes
progress.

I have taken a long walk with my sisters.
I retrace their footsteps
through the roughest terrain.
And with each step, I have grown,
and this growth is shown
in sturdy leg muscles
that emerged out of tussles.

11

Pressure, stress, and duress
forced these legs and feet to go the distance,
and their insistence on persistence –
a desire to finish the race –
has become
their grace.

I have taken a long walk with my sisters,
but I cannot claim
that I have experienced the totality of *their* pain.
Yet, the little bit that I have borne
 has allowed me to gain
some resilience, wisdom,
 and respect for those women
who have endured the worst conditions.

When I think about the long walks of my
sisters...
when I realize that there, but for the grace of
God, go I,
and because of the grace of God,
go I ...
my sisters and I have become
                              one.

4.

Purple Gown

Woman, you are regal in your purple gown.
All that you need now is your crown,
to decorate a mind
 that is more precious than ruby and pearl...
You were once just an ordinary girl...
barely seen...
and now you arrive before the court as Queen.
May the Lord, God continue to hold you
in high esteem.
May the Most High bless you and keep you,
because blessed are the meek... too.
Your humility has granted you the ability to rise
in the presence of doubtful eyes.
Certainly, your low estate has made you great.
Woman, you are regal in your purple gown,
and never again, shall you hold
your dear head down.

Your garments are grand...
and may you stand...
Tall
knowing all...
is well in the peaceful kingdom
of your soul.

5.

Home with Her

I am a woman now,
but I am glad that I still live at home with her,
and she is still at home with me.
She was even younger than I am now
when her mother returned

Home.

I am twenty-five.
She was twenty-two.
How she survived those tender years,
I do not ever want to know...

because
I want her here with me
after my hair becomes as silver as hers.

When I was younger,
I do not remember being this close with her.
Maybe, it is because
I am a woman now.
Now, we talk for hours daily.
Our dialogue is mostly about
God,
and men,
and how to survive... men... with God.

I listen keenly to her morning sermons.
A few verses from the Bible always go well with
breakfast.
In between her sharing daily bread with me,
I watch her as she takes breaks
to sip hot cocoa and nibble on cream of wheat and
yogurt.

It seems that I need her instruction now
more than I ever did before.
Maybe, it is because
I am a woman now.

How she has survived these tender years,
I *do* want to know.

She is a few years shy of sixty now.
She is surviving.
She is coping,
and she continues hoping.

Her life has had its challenges –
many of which, she has shared with me in story,
and many of which, I have witnessed with my
own eyes and ears.

I do believe –
many years from now –
when she does
finally

return

Home,

she will be satisfied.

I do believe this.
Maybe, it is because
I am a woman now.

6.

In the Garden

A.

Mom and I in the garden...
this is our time of fellowship...
communing with one another
and the rest of creation...
all of us in worship of the Great One who made
us.

I am free in this place.

We work hard... turning the earth... and
planting... and watering...
but the labor is sweet.

16

I wear a multicolored scarf tied around my mind...
It contains the rainbow of colors that I see in the garden.

The sun and the toiling under it heat my body, and sweat forms on my head...
My tightly coiled hair – kept in cornrows or twists – drinks in the moisture and draws itself closer to me.

I am dressed in my comfortable, green, three-quarter length baggy linen pants...
Every now and then a breeze comes by and flows up my pant legs...

I have on my black, open back garden clogs. I slip them off from time to time when I want to feel the earth on my bare feet...
I must look closely to distinguish where I and the earth separate.

My skin has been painted a deeper shade of brown from the sun's brush strokes.

B.

My mom...
She's an artist.
She paints beautiful portraits of people...

17

She finds beauty even when beauty is hard to see.
She searches deeply.
She digs, and digs, and digs.... until she finds
something.
I am convinced by her discovery.

My mother is an artist. The garden is one of her
masterpieces:

flowers...
like roses, lilies, hastas, hydrangeas, daisies,
black-eyed susans, and chrysanthemums...
and I only mention a few.
trees...
like Japanese maple and evergreens...
and fruit-bearing ones like apple and nectarine...
and I only mention a few.
bushes...
like blueberry and 'wine and roses' and butterfly
bushes...
and I only mention a few.

vines...
like grape, clematis, and wisteria...
and I only mention a few.

vegetable crops...
like tomatoes, eggplant, collard greens, bell
peppers, and string beans...
and I only mention a few.

All of this organized into a yard garden that is about a quarter of an acre.

C.

My mom often recounts how our backyard was mostly nothing but gravel and a few spots of clay soil when she first moved into our house.

With her hoe, trowel, shovel, and rake...
purchasing seeds and plants...
little by little...over the years...
she got the garden that she has always wanted.
She's acquired knee pains, back aches, and sore shoulders...
but she got the garden that she has always wanted.

D.

My mom testifies that God gave her this garden.
God gave her the strength to work in it.
God allowed the sun and the rain to make it grow.
As a fervent disciple, I watch, learn, and take in all that I can about the garden.

Perhaps, the garden will be my ministry someday too.

7.

"You can call me 'Aunt'"

My sister is pregnant.
I will have a niece by next spring.
In April... there will be new warmth and her.

This is my sister's first child.
I have no children, but I do hope to have some...
someday.
But... to be someone's aunt... the feeling is
almost as splendid as the thought of giving birth
to my own. What a pleasure it is witness the
coming of this new person who is, in some ways,
an extension of me as well...
My sister and I live in the same home, so I am
able to observe her everyday. What a marvel it is
to see her petite, 5'2" frame expand to prepare
this new life.

She is the first pregnant woman that I have had
the opportunity to study like this... up close and
intimately. My   mother   only   had   us   two
daughters, and I am the youngest.

I look at the globe growing inside my sister's
abdomen, and I am astounded by the mini
universe called her womb, where my niece is
developing. I touch the bulging area, and it is so

tight, filled to the brim with the mother's ocean that surrounds my niece's tiny body.

My sister is about five months pregnant now. She is starting to feel my niece squirming around and stretching her newly formed limbs.

I ask my sister what the movement feels like inside of her. She explains to me how it reminds her of popcorn kernels blooming into white, fluffy flowers as they cook in the microwave oven or on the stove. She is feeling the pops and bursts of this new wonderful being.

The family... especially my sister, my mother, and I... eagerly await my niece's arrival. I am sure that she will be an extraordinary addition to this line of women from which we come.

When I finally meet her in the spring, I look forward to introducing myself.

"Hello, there" I will say to her. "You can call me 'Aunt

PART THREE
In Random Rhapsody.

1.

Can you hear my soul's sound?

Can you hear my soul's sound?
Its outcry elevates,
echoes,
and reverberates.

Can you hear my soul's sound?
It cries out for company
 in the chords
of its
melody.

Can you hear my soul's sound?
It waits to wrap itself
around harmony
in a supersonic
symphony!

2.

Fruit Juice

Thoughts can encircle one's mind
like the toughest rind
of a sweet orange, sour lemon, or even the
bitterest lime.

And from time to time,
one may find
that the juices flow together
and make a fruitful rhyme.

3.

Star Gazing

Gazing up at star-lit night,
searching for a sign,
twinkling is my trail of light,
for a destiny divine.

An ebony sky rushes onward with life,
its conclusion I cannot see,
but I remain a loyal wife
trusting in my husband, eternity.

4.

The Winged Brain Part I

 If I had wings on my brain, I would let it fly far
away from here.
I would let it take to the air,
and allow it to escape my share
of despair.
My winged brain would master aviation.
It would sumptuously sail through the currents of
imagination,
finally arriving at its beloved destination...
that numinous place called
          Jubilation.

5.

The Winged Brain Part II

When she's at her best, the winged brain writes.
she writes... and she writes...
until she is able to capture light
in words.
Then she emulates her relatives, the birds,
soaring out the darkness.

She is light.
She is absent of darkness.

24

She is light.
She is weightless.
She no longer carries a heavy load.
She is wait-less.
She waits less for change.
She just writes...
and that makes her happy.

6.

My Eyes

My eyes are brown
because they were formed from the blessed
ground.
They are in the image of fruitful earth
which gave me birth.
My eyes are golden
because they are like the sun that emboldens
all of creation
with its animating rays.

My eyes are green
because they reflect the screen
of fertile landscape.

My eyes are blue
because they are the hue
of bountiful sky.

25

My eyes are red
because they have bled
the nourishing liquid of the vein.
Yet, they are also red like the flame
that ignites the light of life,
and also sends it back to

dust.

7.

I like to ride my bike

I like to ride my bike.
I like the tickle of the cool wind
on my skin.

I like to ride my bike.
I like to ride, and ride, and ride...
until all of my problems roll away
like the pavement that's now behind me.

I like to ride my bike.
I like to ride so fast that I feel like I am afloat...
like a little boat
drifting...
 in the middle of nowhere.
I am suspended there
without a care.

In this place, I am no longer earthbound,
and the troubles that I face when my feet are
touching the ground
are not my mine now.

I like to ride my bike.
I like the burn of the smoldering sun
on my skin,
and the burn in my legs as I turn the pedals.
It makes me feel like I am a rebel,
rising up against the pain.

I like to ride my bike.
I like to ride, and ride, and ride...
until I glide...
and everything's
easy.

8.

An afternoon stroll

When nature's afternoon feast teases,
my famished heart pleases
the platter of its plenty –
and with my eyes,
I kiss the sun gently.

I taste its ribbon of light rays,

27

and the flavor resembles sweet syrup
falling from warm lips.

The sweetness drips...
until it drenches me.

I take a few more dips
in this solar bath,
and while traveling along my path
I ingest the best of fresh air, sight, and sound.

By the end of my stroll, I find that I am round,
satiated from all the afternoon goodness.

9.

About the Seasons

Winter, spring, summer, fall.
Which is the best season of them all?
I dare not try to make a decision,
because each season yields its own splendid vision.
Winter brings fields of glorious, sparkling white
cotton
upon lush green earth now forgotten.
But the foliage and flora return with the dawning
of spring,
and the resurgence of life is witnessed in many a
thing.

28

Then radiant summer makes the sweet and savory
ripe for the picking,
but high times won't last forever,
as nature's clock is ticking.
Fall soon comes with resolute calmness and
certain tranquility,
giving all a time of rest and stability.
Yet its landscape is still as impressive as seasons
past,
adorning colors of fiery orange, burnt sienna, and
royal scarlet –
a sight that would be un-regrettably the year's
last.
But there is always a chance of early winter chill
before the next year is scheduled to start.
So we retreat indoors, just to be smart.
After all is said and done,
there is always pleasure and beauty to experience
under the mighty sun.
Whether the day is hot and dry, or wet and cold,
there is always a precious story about it that has
yet to be told.
You could have a celebration of winter over hot
cocoa or tea,
or perhaps you prefer your tea iced – or you enjoy
sipping lemonade
in the summer shade.
Either way, every season has a guarantee to
titillate and stimulate
the grateful eyes that behold the marvels of
creation.

And it is a joyful sensation and a satisfying
revelation
to discover that everything has its season,
and everything has a reason
for being.
So let us open our eyes and begin seeing
everything that God has designed.
After all, everything has been assigned and given
its specific time.

Summer, fall, winter, spring,
I only await the wonders that each season is
destined to bring.

10.

"How 'bout them apples…?"

"How 'bout them apples…?"
says the soul that grapples
with life's challenges.
Instead of swallowing sour defeat,
go eat something sweet.

"How 'bout them apples?

PART FOUR
Solos for the "So-Lows".

1.

Word Power

I have watched my dreams
dissipate into streams of nothingness —
and now, without a doubt, I shout out
that I expect nothing less
than a miracle.
Inside of my mind there is a lyrical calamity.
It is a verbal chaos with a contradictory mission
 to restore my sanity.
I have heard that
out of the darkness comes the light,
and out of blindness comes sight.
Out of nothing comes something profound.
I am a listener, and so I search for the sound.
Although some may think it absurd,
I believe that paradise exists in
a word.
And through the power of a word... a single
word...
I can effect change...   "Yes."

31

2.

Boredom colonizes the hopeless mind

Boredom colonizes the hopeless mind.
Nowhere to go... nothing to find.
No conquest left to possess in my dreams.
This reality is tainted – nothing is quite what it
seems.

Boredom colonizes the hopeless mind.
No one to jog your memory about the happy
times.
Damn amnesia – what is only recalled is every
wish resigned.
Where is the bonfire to thaw my frozen limbs and
illuminate my vision
in this cold and dark wilderness, with the signate,
"life"?
I cannot see for the trees,
I could cut them all down if I had a knife.
"So why don't you cut them all down, and claim
this region as your very own?"
Those voices, they speak to you and tempt you in
the wilderness,
when you're idle and alone.
"You are no one", they say. "Just another useless,
uncultivated mind... just another ugly face...just
another body of matter taking up space."
Boredom colonizes the hopeless mind.
No one else seems to care about seeing,

32

so why don't I stay selfishly blind?
Why do anything, if I can do nothing and still
live?
Generosity just sucks the life out of you.
You die like a slave as you give and give.
I can follow the blueprint of empire –
Either 'exploit', or 'be exploited',
either furnish your own, or be consumed by
someone else's fire.

Boredom colonizes the hopeless mind.
I am tired of doing nothing –
Now it's time to unwind.

3.

Mountains

We all encounter mountains.
The mountains about which I speak
are the towering obstacles
that obstruct our mobility.

We don't climb these mountains;
these mountains climb on us.
These mountains climb on our spines,
applying excessive pressure to our vertebrae.

They climb… and they climb…

until the weight of them is so burdensome
that they paralyze our bodies.

In order to liberate our limbs,
we must throw these mountains off
our backs.
Then, we may move again.

4.

at the river's edge – Psalm 46

i sit by the river's edge, contemplating this
drought in my life.
the emptiness inside – it pierces like a knife.
razor sharp nothingness boring a hole in my soul,
i sit by the river's edge, waiting for God to
replenish my cup and bowl.
i pray that He fills them high with the milk and
honey of His promise,
the temptation of tribulation attempts to make
me a doubting thomas.
doubting God's faithfulness, mercy, and grace,
holding on, i look up towards the heavens, at the
Almighty's face.
that is, the afternoon sun, which behaves briefly
as a balm for my wounds,
and for a moment, i believe that rescue is coming
soon.

i sit by the river's edge, and i could almost jump
in,
i imagine i'm a fish with sturdy fins.
they balance, propel, and steer me through the
rapidly flowing streams,
i don't have this sense of direction as a human it
seems –
that intuitive wisdom which tells me which way is
right,
has God disconnected me from it for a period of
night?
it is night now in my life, for i only see the
darkness,
i feel the void, and i can taste the starkness.
it tastes of dust flakes so bitter and dry, and
stinging in my eye,
i sit by the river's edge, hoping that the water will
at least allow me to cry.
the loss of feeling is so great that i cannot even
muster up a tear,
if i get a little mist in my eyes perhaps my vision
will be a bit more clear.
clear – like the river's undulating waves which
flow to and fro,
flowing forward into perpetuity, with a conclusion
my finite sight will never know.
but i only pray, that amidst the rush,
that i can get a glimpse of my own reflection,
in the surging waters so vast and lush,
i seek an image with which i can make a
connection.

i sit by the river's edge, and then suddenly i
happen to see,
amongst all the movement and uncertainty,
something still, something stable – something
that looks a lot like...
Me.
i run my fingers through the water's surface so
that, in a touch,
the image and i can become one.
and i realize, that, above us both, is still the
afternoon sun.
its rays descend upon the water, emitting
particles of light,
particles dancing around in different colors like a
rainbow, shimmering bright.
i sit by the river's edge, hoping that it will quench
the thirst of my grief,
so I take a sip of my own reflection, and i find
that it provides a little relief.
my cup and bowl are not overflowing yet, but
perhaps i am beginning to see them refill.
i sit by the river's edge... the edge of life...
and at that moment when i am ready to jump in...
i am reminded to be...
still.

5.

at the clearing

i was ...
misplaced, displaced, disgraced
dejected, neglected, rejected, subjected to
madness –
searching for the antidote to
cure me of this chronic sadness.
this cancer – so malignant and indignant,
it was demolishing the very core of my existence.
and my soul yearned to know resistance...
yet i bowed down at the feet of the beast,
and the wind carried rumors of a
tempest coming at me towards the east...
and right at that pinnacle moment
when i thought i had met my demise –
the celestial bodies opened up
with the parting of the nebulous skies
and the emergence of ethereal sunrise.
the warm rays beamed down,
penetrating the disease in my chest,
and like the healing hands of a nurturer
they caressed and suppressed
the agony in my sickly heart.

6.

Re-Breath (Rebirth)

Mommy, i'm tired of living
because living is starting to feel a lot like death,
i went to let go,
so i am frantically holding my breath...
frantically holding my breath...
hoping... just waiting for there to be – of this life
– nothing left.
Left – why do i keep on going left?
i desperately need something to be right.
my eyes are swollen from the waterfalls that flood
my face at night.
It must be in my sleep
that i perpetually weep.
But i cannot explain...
i don't remember this pain
in my waking hours,
i have become numb, and i can no longer feel the
showers.
i cannot feel the showers of blessing, nor the
showers of sorrow,
my God, my God, i am so, so sorry that i cannot
see a reason for my tomorrow.

Daddy, i'm tired of living
because living is starting to feel a lot like death,
i just want to end it all,
so i am frantically holding my breath...

frantically holding my breath, waiting for the
minutes to disappear...
my heart starts pounding in anticipation and fear,
fear that i may be committing an unforgivable
sin,
putting my life to an end like this before it ever
even begins.
i know that it hasn't begun yet because i am still
in death.
i know now that you can be dead while you are
sipping in breath after breath,
drinking in the noxious air of the world,
the expense of the treachery, the tyranny, the
drudgery, the agony,
my spirit can no longer afford.
But i have heard that there is a Savior, who came
and paid the cost,
died and found life again so that my soul could be
undead and un-lost.
But my God – why does it feel that you have
forsaken me?
my God, my God, why have you forsaken me?
The desert sands, they have risen high and have
overtaken me.
The hot grains consume me and fill my throat,
i don't have time now to write a goodbye note.
Lord, i was tired of living
because living was starting to feel a lot like death,
i wanted to see life start,
so i frantically held my breath...
frantically held my breath...

frantically held my breath, until i finally slipped away,
slipped away to a place where there was day.
In this place i hear a voice say, "My child, you are ready to begin,
You have been cleansed now... washed away are your sins."

I feel the showers now... flowing upon me like a river,
"Let the waters touch you", the Voice says.
"They wash, they save, they deliver."
The Voice speaks more to me and I concentrate to hear it,
"I tell you the truth; no one can enter the Kingdom of God unless he is born of water and Spirit".
"Who are you" I ask.
"I AM", the Voice replies.
"You are ready now... go ahead and open your eyes."
So I open my eyes and I find myself coughing and gasping for air.
"I have come back... I am still here", I think to myself –
and at the bounty in front of me I stare.
Waterfalls flood my face again,
this time for the joy of another breath,
so I frantically catch my breath, and yet another breath...

Mommy, Daddy...I am ready to live.

7.

The Sign of the Rainbow

My mother says
that a rainbow is
the sign of
God's Promise.
 I often search for it
on the horizon –
in the space between the Heavens and the earth.

A rainbow forms
when the sun's rays
pass through
falling rain or mist.

To me, a rainbow is like
faith.
Even amid sorrow,
the one who possesses faith
still believes that there is a reason for joy.

Just as the sun's rays persevere
through the falling rain,
the one who possesses faith
presses onward
with a smile,

41

passing through the momentary tears.

8.

The Paradox of Triumph

When one deprives me of love,
the more I strive for love,
the more I survive for love,
the more that I must
stay alive for love.

When one sentences me to death,
the more I encourage each breath –
propelling myself into further existence,
because this is my ultimate act of resistance.

When one hopes that I've died
from the inflicted wounds
of pierced heart and side,
much to my enemy's surprise,
I rise.

From the gaping holes
flow forth the blood and water
which animate the life force within.
I've been the victim of sin,
and endured its pain –
and my scars were a stain.
But now they are my beauty mark –
a birthmark that I wear for

42

new life.

Yes, from me flows
blood and water –
a nourishing libation
that I now offer in celebration.

9.

The Release

I was sent away
for a few years.
I had limited contact with others,
and the loneliness brought me tears.

At the time, I thought that isolation was
a tomb,
but I learned that it was
a womb.

Solitary confinement
gave birth to
refinement.

I received a polishing
that produced
the abolishing
of a captive mind.

43

Now, I reenter society
without anxiety,
casting away all qualms.

Who knew that the adjudication
of isolation
would be my liberation?

PART FIVE
Hymns about him.

1.

Singer Man

Let me tell you about how
I love a Singer Man.

It is his voice that encircles me like silk
and if I could articulate its taste, it would be like
mother's warm milk
to a baby crying in the midnight hour,
and now, no longer are my days sour
when I can hear him in my ear.

He opens his mouth and strokes his guitar with
tender fingers,
and I am in a fragrant meadow where the sweet
scent of him lingers...
He is the songbird serenading the flowers,
and irrigating the earth in vocal showers.

Some nights I let his soothing voice rock me to
sleep.

45

As I transition from awake-ness, my soul begins
to leap...
It springs into a dimension where all of my sorrow
flees.
And there is only a gentle breeze
where I hear, smell, and taste his melody.

Jasmine, gardenia, lily, lilac, and rose in my nose,
honeysuckle on the tip of my tongue,
It reminds me of a tune that Miss Roberta and
Miss Lauryn have sung.

But he is doing more than strumming my pain
with his fingers...
 he is numbing my pain with his fingers.
Singing my life with his words.
Oh... singing my life with his words.
Yet he is not killing me softly with his song.
He is *filling* me softly with his song.
Reviving me softly with his song.
Enlivening me softly with his song.

I am so... *alive.*

Let me tell you about how
I love a Singer Man.

I have found
that his appearance is as pleasant as his sound.
He is not without beauty and bounty both inside
and out.

46

Soul and body combine
into something sublime
called
him.

I enjoy his forehead because it stands so broad
and high.
That must be the place where, came to be, that
alluring lullaby.
It's surely the sign of a beautiful mind,
a cradle for love songs – a haven that God
designed.

That is how I love a Singer Man.

2.

Is this young man...?

Is this young man to be mine?
Is he the one assigned
To hold my hand through the epochs etched in
Time – ?
And like a prized diamond
Will our union become more brilliant and radiant
With age – ?
And if the Universe is just a stage,
And we are the thespians in this play-drama
called 'life',

Is he my leading man,
And I his leading wife?

Is this young man to be mine?
Is he the one to provide the water and sunshine
To nurture my flower bed
and germinate my seeds – ?
Is his living liquid potent enough
To drown out and wash away the weeds – ?
And quench the thirst of a drought of long – ?
And if life is all just one complicated song,
Is he the harmony to my melody –
And together will we progress in perfect, rhythmic
synchronization?
So I had this revelation –
And I would say 'yes' with no hesitation.

Thus the solitary question that is to ensue –
"Is this young man to be... You?"

3.

A Woman's Solitude

Am I that unlovable, un-huggable, un-tuggable?
Un-tuggable – why can't I pull on your
heartstrings?
Strings – do I have too many strings attached –

too many past burdens on my back causing my
garments to fray and detach?
My attire, so unattractively tattered
that I'm almost unclothed, indisposed – my soul
is exposed.
And now you have imposed yet another wound
where there was visible flesh.
Blood is flowing forth from the place where you
have pierced my bare breast.
My breast – my pillow of love on which I intended
to let your mind and spirit rest.
Rest – but I guess the rest is history
and you are yet another mystery –
a mystery of a man, who without explanation,
chose not to take my hand.
Hand – why can't you just hand over the
information
which would clarify your hesitation in pursuing
me?
Is silence better than voicing your disagreement
openly?
Am I simply a woman without eligibility?
If so, I have no more ability to contain the
sorrow.
Is there another's heart, just for a while, that I
could borrow?
Borrow – may I borrow another's heart until I
feel confident in the fortitude of my own heart
again?
Again – will there ever be another again
to put an end

49

to this solitude?

4.

The hummingbird

It has become routine now.

Year after year he hums in my ear,
flittering through my spring and summer garden -
and for those months he was absent,
I grant him pardon.

I admit that each visit is a bit longer than the
last,
but I am convinced that he is bound to behave as
he has in the past.

He sips off the nectar of my emotion,
and my soul endures a commotion
from this temporary devotion.
I want to believe that he is sweet and benign,
because I am captivated by each line he sings
as we cross-pollinate in
conversation.
If I could... I would prolong the sensation.

In an attempt to grab hold of him, I cast my
net...
but as of yet —
he is unattainable.

I resign that this bird will never be trainable,
as he was designed for wild and elusive flight.
I could try with all of my might,
but I don't believe that I could ever make him be
still,
as it appears that he is determined by his own will
to keep his wings in constant motion.

So I must forget the notion
that he plans to perch.
Therefore, I intend to end my search.

I don't plan to pursue him anymore.

5.

In Sweet September...

In sweet September
I won't remember
the season of before.
The lazy runner
of hazy summer
has run her course for sure.

A lonely heart chasing romance,
in a race where love would never advance,
I discover

51

youthful passion
is not a fashion
that I can sport all year long.

I was running from the sorrow of a love rose
which had bloomed in spring,
whose petals fell away too soon...
like a dove who desires flight on a sunny
afternoon...
but is a captive of her clipped wings.

Unable to catch the freshly ripened petals which
floated away upon a breeze,
I desperately sought out another flower which I
had hoped that I would be able to seize.

In May, my love rose was gone...
In June, I believed that I had found a new.
But perhaps it was too late
to germinate
a sentiment just as true.

For my love rose was a product that required
months for its making.
And I had sown sweat, tears, and prayers in this
great undertaking.
In late autumn of year last, I myself had picked
out the seed,
and when it was time for its planting in spring,
I patiently watched it sprout to growth despite
the weeds.

Then my love rose left me
almost as soon as it came.
And I wondered if my poor heart
would ever surpass the pain.

When my love rose was gone,
I found myself in so much grief.
So when I caught sight of another rose,
I wanted it so much to be my relief.

I sniffed the scent of the new rose…
I admit it was not as fragrant to my nose.
But consumed by a burning in the early summer
heat…
I convinced myself, for a while, that the aroma
was just as sweet.
Cautious by nature, I didn't dare pluck the rose
from the bush,
but its fairness did indeed give my imagination a
push.

I caressed the petals and gently embraced its
thorny stem…
and I found some pleasure in this little game of
love pretend.

Yet still living inside of me was a yearning
unfulfilled…
A feeling that I'd hoped had died in me still
remained 'un-killed'.

53

In July, I cry...
and struggle with my little lie.
In August, I know...
that I must eventually let the new rose go...

Then comes September... sweet September,
and we finally go our separate ways.
I am still caught up in the whirlwind
of a sultry summer daze.

I am a bit tipsy off the wine
of frivolous times,
but will I have to wait until October
to become sober?

Will the cool of autumn
make my heart numb?
Or do I make preparation
for a true love that is to come?

Strolling in my garden of possibility,
I survey the open space.
I'll take my time before I pick out a new flower,
because I know now that there is so much waste
in haste.

In sweet September
I still remember
the spring of before.
I still remember

a love rose so tender
that I had grown to adore.

In sweet September
I still remember
late autumn of year last.
And can my heart surrender
to a new contender
that will comfort me from the past?

Oh sweet September...
sweet, sweet September...
it seems summer could not dismember
the memory of a past warm December.

6.

Reminiscing

Late at night
is when she wishes
it were morning the most,
because she is mourning
over the missing of him.
Perhaps tomorrow
will beget a day to forget
the night's remembrances of yester.

PART SIX
Love Ballads

1.

Endings

There was a flame,
and then it died.
That's how love goes sometimes.
Was it a torrent of tears
or the cold rain
on a burning heart
 that finally put the light out
when I saw the truth?

Only I was afire.

And when that one
for whom I was ablaze
walked past me like a frigid storm,
I knew
that it was the end.

But love is eternal,
and it always seeks and finds new persons, places,
and things
to ignite.

56

2.

Some People, Other People

Some people hate.
Some people hurt.
Some people inflict so much pain on bodies, souls,
and brains by hurling stones, bullets, fiery words,
and flames of rage.
And some people never learn from the burn.

Some people just continue to perpetuate the cycle
of hate. And the hate becomes so great that it is
eventually too late for anymore life.

But…

Because there is a gracious God… there *are* other
people.
There are other people who *do* learn.
There are other people who learn… love.
There are other people who choose love….
who give love, and…

Live.

3.

Favorable Foe

Favorable foe –
I must not desist to resist
the notion of sweet emotion.
I could dismiss the craving of a kiss,
and the chasing of embracing.
I could contest the anticipation of conversation
and the yearning of relation,
but the sensation...
and moreover, the stimulation...
of your essence grows...

Will this desire
overthrow my empire?
Will I be consumed
 by this fire?

As I prepare to lay down my sword and shield on
the battlefield,
and yield...
I remember that this War –
and no matter how powerful the lure,
I refuse to lose.

Pride or Passion?
Why must I choose?

4.

Confession

Love... I must confess it.

You are ... love.

Impossible love, improbable love.
unbelievable love, inconceivable love,
unperceivable love.

You are... love.

Un-dream-able love, un-seem-able love.
unreasonable love, unseasonable love.
illogical love, un-chronological love.

But you are... love.

I say that
this isn't the time and place for love.
I could not picture yours as the face for love.

Unsuspected love, un-projected love.
unplanned love, un-manned love.
 I don't understand this love,
because I didn't have my hands in this love.

Yet, you are... love.

I am so full of doubt, love.
I can't see this working out, love.

You are suspicious love...
but you are un-vicious, love.
I want to say that you don't belong, love,
but I cannot detect any wrong, love.
...And now the feelings are so strong, love.

The how and why you are choosing me, love
is something that's confusing me, love.
But you are truly amusing me, love,
and now I don't think that I want you refusing
me, love.

Is this going to be hard love?
Are you going to leave me scarred, love?

You are acute, love.
You are astute, love.
 I believe that you know how I feel, love,
and I beg you not to steal, love – my fragile
emotions.

But if you are truly love,
you would not hurt me or desert me, love –
you would give me your total devotion.

I have admired you, love,
desired you, love,
but never imagined you as my own.

I believed that
you were untouchable love,
un-clutch-able love,
and I could not cross the threshold into your zone.

You are wild love,
and I feel like a child, love,
when I see the freedom that you hold in your
hands.
Sometimes I watch you soar, love,
and I want to explore, love –
and ascend into your lands.

I could never tame you, love,
or claim you, love,
for I would belong to you.
And now the time has arrived, love,
when I must decide, love.
What are you and I to do?

Love...
For you, I'd have to grow up and show up
because you are... mature love.
You are sure love.
Although you are seasoned, you are pure love.

I admit that I am intimidated by you, love.
Yet, I am also stimulated by you, love.

You are unique, love,
and you have this mystique, love –

a magnetism like no other.

I don't want to be a fool, love,
but you have this pull, love –
and it makes me want to be your lover.

At first, you were unassuming love,
but now you are consuming love –
taking all of me with your presence.

You don't need action, love
to rouse my attraction, love –
I am simply compelled by your essence.

This time I can't deny, love,
that I don't want to say goodbye, love.
So let's give love a try, love.
Let's give love a try.

So, please... don't you leave me in suspense, love.
When will this love commence, love?
When will
this love
commence?

5.

Progression

Before I saw it, I felt it.
Before I felt it, I thought it.
Before I thought it, I knew it.
Before I knew it, I was it.

I was it
because the I AM has always been,
and the I AM allowed me
to be.

I was when it was
then.
And I have been becoming it.
And I AM it
now.

And now, I know
that
you are You.
For have seen it...
felt it...
thought it...
knew it.

You are
because you always were,
and you always have been,

as I AM.

You have been becoming it,
and then you became it,

and now that you are it,

and now that I *know*
that you are it,

You and I

                    ARE.

6.

Turn Around

Hitherto,
my milieu
was a melancholic blue.
Then you came into view
as a shade of euphoric yellow
that brightened up my hue.

7.

It was always meant to be

It was always meant to be
like sand meeting the sea,
like earth greeting a tree
inviting it to make a home in the soil.

It is a friendship so loyal
like the winged life form and sky
as the sky shares sacred space
with the eagle, dove, bee, and butterfly.

It was always meant to be
like a baby suckling mama's breast,
like the sun setting in the west,
then rising again in the east –
breaking earth's fast from light at night
with a brilliant morning feast!

8.

Each one. It's really that simple.

Each one reach one.
Each one teach one.
Each one respect one.
Each one protect one.

65

Each one befriend one.
Each one defend one.
Each one collaborate with one.
Each one celebrate with one.
Each one laugh with one.
Each one share half with one.
Each one smile with one.
Each one spend a while with one.
Each one hear with one.
Each one shed a tear with one.
Each one remain with one.
Each one gain with one.
Each one discern from one.
Each one learn from one.
Each one give for one.
Each one live for one.

9.

This is… about… Love.

This is… about… Love.
Among the most critical misconceptions
about love.
is that we believe that we are *doing* for love.
What is true is quite the opposite.
Love is always doing for us.
Love is always the subject…
and we are always the objects of its action.

By grace, love only sanctions our belief that we are doing and working for it.
Love never needed our work.
While we are yet pursuing love, love has already found us first.
While we are fighting for love, love has already won the battle.
While we are conceiving love, love has already conceived us.
While we are laboring for love, love has already completed the work.
While we are waiting for love, love patiently waits for us to realize that it is already
present.
Love is always present. Love has always been present.
Love will always be… the present.
Love is the gift that is ours eternally.
Our only contribution is the surrendering of our souls to this revelation.
Yet, what is so gracious of love is that it allows us to believe that we are...
working for it.
Love never needed our work.
Love possesses so great a nature of humility that it permits us to believe that we are necessities to its existence.
The truth is, however, that we would not exist without it.
Love is necessary for our existence.

67

Oh, how great love is to relinquish some of its
power to us voluntarily in order to create a sense
of need for us. This need gives us value.
But love never really needed our work.
Yet, what is so gracious of love is that it allows us
to believe that we are...
working for it.
Love does not give us this process of "work" with
intentions to deceive.
Love gives us this process, so that we might...
believe...
believe in its power...
to save... to elevate... to educate... to edify... to
heal...
and to reveal.
Work allows us to appreciate that which we
attain in love.
Love relinquishes some of its power in order that
we might ultimately see its...
Power...
In order that we might ultimately see that it is
the...
Greatest Power.

Indeed, Love never needed our work.

PART SEVEN
Finale

1.

Re-acquaintance

Sometimes I say too much.
Sometimes I say too little.
Sometimes I say nothing at all
when I should have said
everything.

My words often seem to betray me.
I'm trying to find the perfect.
                              Balance.
So I will just start with
"goodbye"
and end with "hello".

These are all of the things
that I should have said
 before.

2.

Movement

Movement.
We are *moving* creatures, and the remnants of our
movement become our legacy.
Footprints in the sand. Palm prints in the soil.
Seraphs in the snow.
Images and inscriptions on stone, and paper, and
canvas, and film, and ingrained in minds.
Tears, and perspiration, and blood, and spittle,
and discharge, and excrement expelled from the
functioning organism.
Aromas from vanished bodies permeating the air.
Trails of sound echoing behind us.
As we traverse through life, we leave portions of
ourselves in our paths.
Sometimes a portion remains in a particular place
and grows. Sometimes a portion travels and
grows.

     Movement.
We are *moving* creatures, and the remnants of our
movement become our legacy.
Sometimes movement becomes a word.
Sometimes a word becomes movements.
Sometimes movements become words. Sometimes
words become stories. Sometimes stories become
knowledge. Sometimes knowledge becomes

70

progress. Sometimes progress becomes evolution.
Sometimes evolution becomes wisdom. Sometimes
wisdom becomes words... and words... words.
And sometimes the words cycle, and recycle, and
proliferate, and mature into
change.

Movement.
We are *moving* creatures, and the remnants of our
movement become our legacy.

3.

Coming to myself

Should I travel on foot? –
I am coming to myself.

Should I take my journey on horseback? –
I am coming to myself.

Should I voyage by carriage or rickshaw? –
I am coming to myself.

Should I cross by canoe or steamboat? –
I am coming to myself.

Should I hop on a bicycle or skateboard? –
I am coming to myself.

71

Should I go by bus or train? –
I am coming to myself.

Should I catch a plane? –
I am coming to myself.

Should I make my trek on a space ship? –
I am coming to myself.

Should I spread out on a magic carpet? –
I am coming to myself.

Should I go through a time machine? –
I am coming to myself.

Should I?.. Should I?... Should I? –
As long as I am coming to myself.

4.

Renovation

We build,
and we break.
We rebuild,
and we break...
And rebuild –
until we make
something stable,

72

something we can label
a proper foundation...
a sound location for love,
a profound station for peace,
furnished with faith
and grounded in truth...

5.

earthquake: the time is at hand

the time is at hand
when the inner murmurings of truth
become the outer mumblings of change.
and these mumblings
escalate into rumblings
that stir up and agitate
the foundations of buildings erected in our youth.

these buildings are grand structures,
man-crafted brick by brick
of falsehoods and lies.
their image eventually becomes
disruptive to the eyes of the wise.

you might ask, 'who are the wise'?
the wise are the misfits, the outcasts, the rejects.
the wise are those who are willing
to disconnect

themselves from a dysfunctional community –
whether it is family or nation,
nation or global generation.
and the hope
is that this disconnection from the community
will produce a greater unity.
and this greater unity
would be the potential opportunity
to become one with the Highest truth.

the wise are not necessarily the best
or above the rest,
the wise are not the elite,
they are simply the elect.
they are the ones chosen to reject
the social order,
which borders on
disorder.

this disorder
is a communicable disease
that travels on the breeze of mass
communication.
on the air waves they are announcing mass
assimilation
which results in identity assassination.

i have been a victim of attempted identity
assassination.
someone has tried to murder who I am.
someone has tried to murder the "I am" in me.

74

that is my original self
which was in the image of my originator
who is the Creator.

in the beginning
i existed in perfect construction,
and persisted without obstruction
until someone disturbed my view
by imposing their views upon me.
i encountered...
historical conditions,
empty human traditions,
social dynamics
that short-circuited my mental mechanics.
and there was many a generational curse...
which attempted to loot my spiritual purse...
that was the wealth of self given to me by the
Most High.

therefore, the time is at hand
when one begins to understand
that only some buildings are built by man
but the One who built all things is God.
and when one's feet become shod
with the gospel of peace,
one experiences a release
from the lies which disguise
and blind the eyes
like buildings that stand so high
that they try
to block out the light of the sun.

so it appears that a new day has begun
when the wise realize that the great towers must
fall
and that there is life and light behind a man-made
wall.

the wise dismantle the buildings progressively and
diligently,
bringing down brick after brick,
and they gradually heal themselves from that
which has made innocent souls sick.

and with courage composing the wick,
the wise boldly hold and light the candle
and kindle the flames of revolution.
the fire this time is the final solution.

first comes the earthquake which causes the
buildings to crumble,
and then the booming blaze completes the
tumble.

the time is at hand.

The beginning.

ABOUT THE AUTHOR

Ms. Tenagne Holland Tessema was born and raised in Ardmore, Pennsylvania. She has been a literature lover since childhood. When Ms. Tessema was a young girl, she became an avid reader and writer of short stories. The author turned to the "poet's pen" during her teenage years, in pursuit of a creative outlet for her adolescent angst. As the years progressed, Ms. Tessema developed an earnest passion for poetry as a form of artistic and personal expression. In her adult years, poetry continues to be a means by which she is able to find great solace and sanctuary for her soul. Poetry is deeply intertwined with her spiritual journey. The author perceives poetry as her time of communion with God.

In addition to writing poetry, Ms. Tessema also has a fervent love for working with children. She is dedicated to serving youths as an elementary and early childhood educator. Ms. Tessema holds a Bachelor of Arts degree in History from Bryn Mawr College in Bryn Mawr, Pennsylvania, and she is currently completing a Master of Science degree in Teaching, Learning, & Curriculum from Drexel University in Philadelphia, Pennsylvania. She continues to live in her hometown of Ardmore.

Made in the USA
Middletown, DE
27 September 2021